DISCOVER ART
Oil Painting

DISCOVER ART
Oil Painting

Mike Chaplin
with Diana Vowles

SELECT
EDITIONS

*Thanks to Gaynor Lloyd for the Bonnard copies on pp. 6
and 25 and for the life drawings on pp. 36 and 37.*

This edition published 2005

Selectabook Ltd
Folly Road, Roundway, Devizes,
Wiltshire SN10 2HT

Cover photography by Thomas Mitchell

ISBN 1-84193-272-8

Printed in Singapore

CONTENTS

INTRODUCTION

Oil painting is probably the most durable form of painting there is; indeed, it often remains in better condition than the surface it has been painted on. It is also extremely liberating, for the work is no longer limited to the size of paper that is produced by a manufacturer; measurements are dictated only by the imagination and energy of the painter. Tintoretto's Paradise (1588--90), to be seen in the Doge's Palace in Venice, is believed to be the largest oil painting in the world at an astonishing 7.6 × 24.6 m (25 × 81 ft).

So the idea of painting in oils is exciting, but it is also challenging. Setting yourself up with the right equipment seems a more complicated

Pierre Bonnard painted many domestic scenes, using what was then the modern manner of showing the activity of painting rather than striving for a high degree of finish (see detail below). Shown here is a copy of *Au coin de salle à manger* (*In the Corner of the Dining Room*), painted in 1932.

and expensive task than acquiring watercolours and paper such as can be found in many high street stationers. More importantly, oil painting seems to carry a greater weight of history, from the Old Masters to the Impressionists and beyond. As an amateur, it is easy to feel that it is the province of 'real' artists.

However, remember that the Impressionists themselves cocked a snook at history and threw aside the high degree of finish that was previously considered essential in favour of pictures that showed the activity of painting, which is how we still paint today. Oil pigments are capable of being worked from the thinnest, most delicate glazes up to the heaviest impastos that are almost sculptural in their relief, and you will be able to find a manner of using them that suits your own capability and temperament – so take pleasure in the excitement of putting paint down and your confidence will grow with practice. You may eventually find you want to paint in the manner of grand narrative works such as George Stubbs (1724–1806) favoured, or the gentle domestic style

My copy of *Lion Attacking a Horse* by George Stubbs shows a grand manner narrative painting full of detailed drawing. The original painting measures not much more than the Bonnard on the facing page, though the drama of the piece makes it seem large in scale.

This detail from my painting *The Grand Canal, Venice* shows the pleasure that can be derived from the rich colours that oil paints offer.

employed by Pierre Bonnard (1867–1947) may appeal more to you. Bonnard's habit was to nail canvas directly to the wall rather than using stretchers, and while this may not be popular in most domestic settings I hope it will encourage you to realize that oil paints are after all an approachable medium that you can treat as you will.

In *Lives of the Artists*, Giorgio Vasari (1511–1574) credits Jan van Eyck (1390–1441) with the invention of the oil painting technique that swept through Europe and is not much changed to this day. This book explains the time-honoured methods of mixing paints and applying them to a surface, which may be wooden panel as used in the 15th century, fabric or even modern MDF board. You will learn how to handle different surfaces such as light on stone and reflections on water, with the painting process detailed to guide you through the difficult barrier of tackling the first brushstrokes on a blank surface. It is my hope that as you work through the book you will feel that you want to go on to further exploration of this wonderful painting medium.

BRUSHES AND PAINTS

BRUSHES

Brushes for oil painting tend to be quite stiff bristle, usually hog, though you can use synthetic fibres or a mixture of the two. Most have long handles because oil paintings tend to be quite large scale, in which case you will need to stand up and position yourself far enough away from the work to see what it looks like overall. For detail or fine linework you will want to move in closer, when you will use a short-handled sable brush.

Sable rigger

For use in linework, either flicked lightly, holding the brush at the end, or drawn along the length of the sable bristles.

Bristle stencil brush

Use to scrub on paint. Because the bristles are very short and hard, small lines remain visible. Alternatively, stab the brush repeatedly on the paper to make stippled marks.

Fan or blending brush

Hold the brush very lightly and draw back and forth across the paint to blur the edges where colours meet.

Flat brush

As with an italic pen, pull sideways for a thin mark or downwards for a thick one.

Filbert

Filberts fall between flat and round brushes. They have a curved tip that allows you plenty of control.

PAINTS

Paints all come from the same pigments and it is the binder used with them that determines the medium. In the case of oil paints this is linseed oil. They are available in artists' quality and, more cheaply, students' quality. As the difference between them is quite subtle, I recommend starting out with students' colours so that you won't worry about the cost of experimentation.

If you find the myriad tubes of paint in art shops intimidating, try making your own. I find that my students are much more relaxed about handling pigment that they have ground down with oil themselves, using a muller on a glass slab or a pestle and mortar.

Oil paints are thinned with more linseed oil or, for thin glazes or a matt finish, pure turpentine – not turps substitute, which is for cleaning brushes only. If you don't like the smell of turpentine, you can now buy an odourless substitute called Sansodor.

SUPPORTS

The first traditional supports for oil paints were wood and vellum, with fabrics being a later arrival. Any surface will take paint, but the ones you are most likely to encounter are hessian, canvas, linen, cotton, muslin and MDF board, with the latter being particularly popular.

STRETCHING

Fabrics are stretched on wooden bars, which you can buy in pairs from art shops in various lengths, along with triangular wedges. The longer ones have a slot for a centre bar for extra support. Stretch the fabric round to the back of the frame, staple it to the wood and then knock two wedges into each corner to stretch the fabric taut.

PRIMING

Art shops sell ready-primed canvas, board and textured paper, but other than these you will need to prime all surfaces yourself to prevent the paint sinking into them. The easiest means of doing this is to buy acrylic primer. Begin by laying a thin coat, diluted half and half with water. When that is dry, lay full-strength coats, waiting for each to dry, until the surface will not absorb any more. The number of coats you will need depends on the porosity of the surface, so just continue until the support is no longer visible.

You can lay the primer smoothly or scumble it to give a textured surface that will go through to the paint. You can also add a cool or warm tint, using acrylic paint.

Hessian

Fine cotton

Fine linen

Cotton muslin

Coarse linen

Primed textured paper

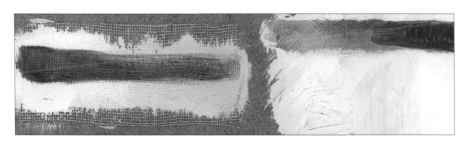

Here I have glued muslin to MDF with primer. On the left, the muslin shows through the primer and will be reflected in the paint quality. On the right, I have added extra coats. Some of this area is smooth, to give a surface on which I can paint accurate lines, while some is scumbled to give texture.

A TRAVEL KIT

While pigments themselves are not flammable the solvents needed for their use as oil paints are, so you may find that you are not allowed to take them on aeroplanes. If you are travelling by air and don't want to risk confiscation of your art materials, the safest choice is the artisan paints made by Winsor & Newton, which are oil paints that you can thin with water. These are of course equally useful at home if you want to avoid using turpentine.

For a neat travelling kit, you can buy pochade boxes in various sizes. They open up to reveal a little flap that acts as an easel, behind which you can store your supports. I stock mine with pieces of ready-primed MDF board.

A pochade box has a central flap that acts as an easel and also keeps your paints and brushes separate from your supports. You can buy neat little containers for oil and turpentine that clip on to the side of the pochade box.

Oil paintings take a long time to dry, so you will often need to transport them while they are still wet. To do this, get four little pieces of dowel from a do-it-yourself shop, hammer a nail into each end and then cut off the head of the nail with pliers. Pin a dowel into each corner of the painting, then put another canvas on top so that the two are held safely apart from each other, face-to-face. You can sometimes buy these dowels from art shops, but it is very easy to make them yourself.

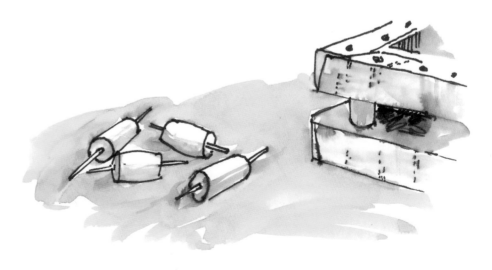

A STUDIO SET-UP

Oil paints are not forgiving if you trample them into the carpet, so you will need to find a permanent painting space where you can lay dustsheet, plastic or cardboard on the floor. Because you will be using oil and turpentine, this must be somewhere there is good ventilation. Ideally, it should have north light so that glare and shadows are not a problem on sunny days. For working after dark, buy some daylight bulbs which mimic natural light.

You will need an easel, either on a stand or a tabletop model. The latter are considerably cheaper and will be adequate for most purposes. If you are showing people your paintings with a view to selling them, putting them on easels is a good way to display them rather than stacking them on the floor.

Paint kettles for cleaning brushes are available from do-it-yourself stores and art shops. The latter supply more sophisticated models with a mesh basket on which you rub your brushes so that all the old paint drops through into the bottom of the kettle. They often have a handle like a big spring which you can wedge your brushes into.

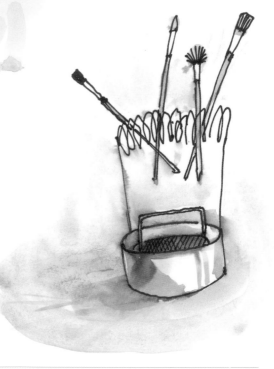

PALETTE LAYOUT AND BASIC MARKS

You will need some sort of palette to keep your paints on. Square or rounded wooden palettes with thumbholes are available from art shops, but if you are on a budget you can make do with a piece of wood or even plastic on a table top. On your palette you will need the colours of the spectrum, usually in both a warm and cool version, plus the earth colours (browns), black and white. Titanium White is opaque, while Flake White is more transparent.

How you lay out your palette is a matter of personal choice. One convention often used for landscape painting is to have dark cool colours one end, light colours in the middle and dark warm colours the other end, with the earth colours separate. Shown below is the layout I prefer.

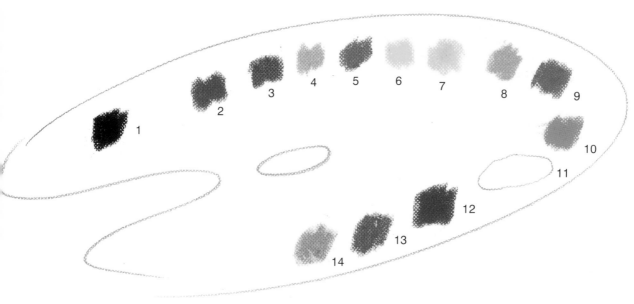

1. Black
2. Ultramarine Violet
3. Ultramarine
4. Light Cobalt
5. Phthalo Green
6. Lemon Yellow
7. Cadmium Yellow
8. Cadmium Orange
9. Alizarin Crimson
10. Cadmium Red
11. White
12. Burnt Umber
13. Raw Umber
14. Terracotta

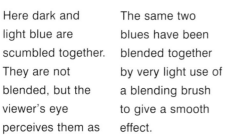

Here dark and light blue are scumbled together. They are not blended, but the viewer's eye perceives them as a single tone with a textural finish.

The same two blues have been blended together by very light use of a blending brush to give a smooth effect.

The dark blue has been laid at the top then pulled out and diluted with linseed oil. This way of changing tone from dark to light gives transparent colour.

Using a palette knife to ladle the paint on gives a thick impasto surface.

A darker colour has been laid on top of a lighter base by scumbling (working the brush with a rotary motion).

Lighter tones have been scratched out with the end of the brush handle, a technique known as *sgraffito*.

Dark blue has been scumbled over the top of light ochre to leave small light marks showing through.

Light green has been scumbled over the top of dark green so the dark marks show through.

These two colours are exactly the same tone so the colours shimmer in relation to each other.

LIFTING OFF PAINT

Removing paint is just as valid a way of mark-making as putting paint down. Shown below are three methods of achieving this. Together with the other techniques of mark-making shown on these pages, they cover nearly all the marks you will encounter in painting.

Paint has been lifted off by laying a sheet of kitchen towel over it and then drawing on the back with a fingernail to blot it off.

A cotton bud can be used as an absorbent pad to lift out colour by drawing into it. If it doesn't come off easily, soak the cotton bud in oil or turpentine.

Here paint has been lifted off by simply twisting a piece of rag into it.

Using glazes

The above illustration shows how you can use cool and warm glazes (transparent layers of paint) to make an area appear remote or intimate respectively. Use glazes with discretion, as they can produce a muddy effect unless you are laying just one pure colour over another. The paint beneath must be absolutely dry.

SKETCHBOOKS AND FORMATS

You will need sketchbooks in two different formats, and although unprimed cartridge paper will suffice for drawing and temporary oil sketches, a pad with primed paper is necessary for permanent oil studies. The advantage of unprimed paper is that the paint dries more quickly, but as it sinks into the paper the quality is poor and oil seeps through the fibre. For more considered sketches I buy books with heavy handmade paper and prime it myself.

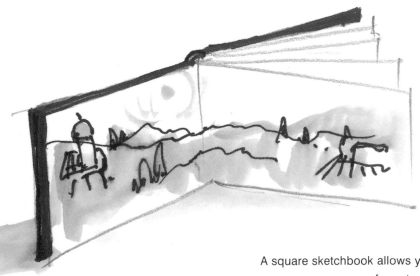

One page of a horizontal panoramic sketchbook gives you a wide landscape format or a portrait format if you turn it sideways. Working across both pages gains you a format of almost four squares, ideal for expanses of landscape.

A square sketchbook allows you a one-page square format or a double square panorama if you use both pages.

Squaring up

When you want to translate a sketchbook composition into a finished painting it is essential to retain the same format. This is done by squaring up.

This pen and wash sketch of a harbour has been squared up by drawing centrally placed horizontal and vertical lines and then drawing diagonals from corner to corner and from the horizontal to the vertical points. The diagonals cross at the middle point of the whole picture and at the middle of each rectangle created by the horizontal and vertical lines.

Put your sketchbook in the bottom lefthand corner of your support. Lay a ruler across it up to the righthand corner and draw a line. Any lines drawn from the side or bottom of the paper to meet on the diagonal will give you the same format.

Referring to your original sketch, you can transfer the elements within it to your support. The two lamp posts pass exactly through the middle of the bottom quadrants, while the top of the harbour wall is exactly on the central horizontal line.

Here I have begun laying in the first loose washes of colour. You can see that the delicate squaring up lines, drawn with a very soft pencil, are already beginning to disappear beneath the paint.

SKETCHBOOK STUDIES

Take a sketchbook with you wherever you go so that you are constantly recording the world around you, building up a visual vocabulary at the same time as you practise your skills. Your sketches may be linear notes or may perhaps contain colour too. Even in monochrome sketches it is always worth putting in the tonal values so that you can see how the light is affecting all the elements of the scene.

My little pen sketch of some figures sitting under a canopy at a Mediterranean café took less than five minutes to do, with some water brushed on to give tone. This is a vignette with no attempt at choosing a composition.

I followed up the pen sketch with a loose colour study, giving more thought to the composition and putting in the cars. If I wish to make a finished painting I now have all the information I need to do so.

There's no need to look for a specific view before you get out your sketchbook; I had fun sketching this little pottery figure in a garden.

This is a more finished sketch of a police station in a Minorcan town. It occupies two pages of the sketchbook and I have put much more thought as to where objects are placed within that shape.

From the drawing above I have begun a small painting of the police station. Note how at this very early stage the colours are already recurring in different areas of the painting to provide unity and dark tones have been put in from which to judge the level of the midtones.

This sketch of the customs house in the same Minorcan town was a brief essay into colour. I used unprimed paper so that the sketch dried within 15 minutes in the hot climate and I could shut my sketchpad and go on my way.

TONE

Tone represents shades from dark to light. In the case of black to white the intermediate tones are a series of greys, and their relationship to each other in terms of which are light and which are dark is easy to discern. With colour, tones become a little more complicated, since strong colours can be confused with dark tones.

Extremes of tone are dramatic, but very close-toned paintings are also interesting as the relationships become about pure colours side by side.

Because the blue and red are strong, pure colours they stand out from the other colours in the panel.

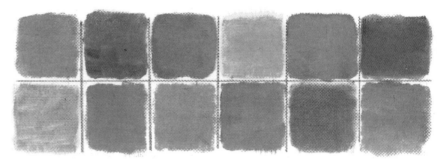

Seen in monochrome, the colours are very similar tonally. The darkest are the muted green and brown.

The strong colours shown above range from light to dark in tone.

Contre jour (against the light) paintings have high tonal drama as backlit objects are thrown into silhouette. The light marks here are achieved by leaving the paper white.

MICHAEL CHAPLIN

This oil study is of some brilliant light on a patch of grass. In comparison to the monochrome sketch on the facing page, the light areas were painted by using light marks on dark so that they become the main focus of attention.

It is not possible to determine a tone until it is seen against another one. Against white paper the tone of this apple looks too dark; by putting a strong dark tone next to it I have made it appear lighter. Putting in the darkest tones at the start of a painting allows you to judge the level of the midtones.

COLOUR

The three primary colours – blue, red and yellow – cannot be mixed from other colours. However, mixed with each other they produce what are called the secondary colours: blue and red make purple, red and yellow make orange, and blue and yellow make green. The colour wheel shown here is made up of the spectrum of colours seen in a rainbow, with the secondary colours between the primaries from which they are made. The colours that face each other across the wheel are opposite, or complementary, to each other. The dark brown in the centre of the wheel is what results if all the primaries are mixed together.

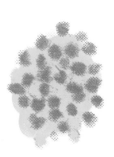

Blue and yellow have been physically mixed together to make green.

When blue and yellow are put down together in small patches, the eye reads them as green from a distance of about 1.8 m (6 ft).

Blue mixed with yellow can never produce a dark-toned green. One way to achieve this is to mix black and yellow.

This little painting, done on the spot, is about using simple colours. It has a freshness that comes from the colour being laid down in one go and then being left alone.

MIXING GREYS

Rather than diluting black, artists tend to make subtle greys by mixing opposite colours. These can either be warm greys, or cool, recessive greys that give a sense of distance.

Grey mixed from yellow and violet.

Greyish-black mixed from green and red.

Grey mixed from orange and blue.

Delphi from the Amphitheatre
101.5 x 152.5 cm (40 x 60 in)
The thrust of this painting is the mixing of opposite colours to produce a very close-toned work. Light is shown by painting some areas of pure colour and some subtle greys made by mixing yellows and purples.

The pillars are painted by laying glazes of light violet over ochre. The viewer sees through one colour to its opposite, so the effect is translucent grey.

In the far-distant mountains, I laid down ochre paint then scumbled violet blue over the top to give an opaque grey.

PERSPECTIVE

SINGLE-POINT PERSPECTIVE

Perspective affects the way we see the world and we need to employ it in our paintings to give a three-dimensional appearance to a two-dimensional piece of board or canvas. While dealing with perspective can be challenging, particularly where archictecture is concerned, a few basic rules will help you through the early stages of learning.

The Fish Market in Venice
101.5 x 152.5 cm (40 x 60 in)
The single-point perspective in this painting leads to the distant building with the light shining on it. My viewpoint was from directly opposite the figure wearing a red shirt.

The overhang of the roof on the right of the distant building creates a little dark triangle that gives volume to the building and leads the eye back down to the vanishing point.

In single-point (or one-point) perspective, parallel lines running directly away from you will converge towards a vanishing point on the horizon. The horizon is always at your eye level.

TWO-POINT PERSPECTIVE

When an object is set obliquely to you, there are two vanishing points. They may not necessarily appear in the frame, but you must understand where they would fall.

V.P. 1   V.P. 2

This diagram shows tables standing obliquely to your viewpoint. Rather than stretching ahead, the lines of perspective converge on the horizon off to the side.

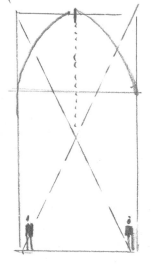

To draw an arch, place it within a rectangle. Draw diagonals in the rectangle. They will cross in the centre, and projecting a line up to the top of the rectangle from that point will give you the spot where the centre of the arch is.

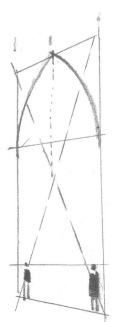

Once the arch is seen in perspective, its highest point is no longer in the centre. Using the same method of drawing diagonals, you will find it about a third of the way along.

Looking at the arches from an angle of about 45 degrees, each one is diminishing about one-third in size as they recede. Note how the lefthand rising side of the arch is a shallow curve seen against the much shorter and tighter curve on the right.

ESTABLISHING SPACE

Linear perspective is not the only way to establish space; you can also use your handling of line, tone and colour. Hard edges, dark tones and warm colours come forward in a painting, while soft edges, pale tones and cool colours recede. As detail becomes less clear the viewer assumes it to be further away, equating it to what is less clearly visible in real life. Likewise, as we look towards a distant view we see aerial perspective causing pale tones of cool blue.

When we look at this block of vertical lines they all seem to be occupying a slightly different place in space. This is achieved by the strength of tone and line and the temperature of the colour.

As this water was painted on midtone blue paper the overall tone has not altered. However, the foreground waves are defined with hard edges and dark tone. At the back they are just insignificant little dashes.

The Palazzo Balbi in Evening Light
101.5 x 152.5 cm (40 x 60 in)

In this painting you can see the effects of using tone to create distance. The foreground is dark in tone, while the buildings in the middle distance are midtone and the Palazzo in the distance is lighter, even in the colour of the roof.

This series of stripes illustrates the phenomenon of aerial perspective. The eye reads that the pale-toned cool blue stripe is the furthest away.

In this detail taken from *View from a Window* by Pierre Bonnard, warm roofs are set against a cool blue distant landscape – a very simple device that gives a feeling of peace and light.

Palazzo Balbi, Afternoon Sun
30.5 x 51 cm (12 x 20 in)

In this second view of the Palazzo Balbi in Venice, the dark jetty just in front of our feet brings the foreground even further forward.

AN URBAN LANDSCAPE

Novice painters tend to put in all the detail at an early stage of a painting and then find it difficult to change it if the work starts to go off track. This project shows you how to embark on a large, complicated painting by working from the general to the specific, so that the structure of the painting is well established at the outset. Investigating your subject by laying in simple areas of colour and tone first makes the work far less daunting to tackle.

First of all I made a quick watercolour study of this well-known and much-painted view of the Basilica in Venice. My aim was just to get the feel of where the light was coming from and where the main areas of architecture were going to be in the composition. The vanishing point is almost halfway up the picture.

In this oil study I moved the horizon line down to divide the picture into thirds horizontally. I also changed my line of vision slightly to bring the whole of the campanile into the picture and included a little bar of the building on the right. This viewpoint divided the picture into thirds vertically – a classic compositional device.

Having established the angle of light and the composition, I began work on the painting by laying in the first areas of tone. Putting in the darkest tone, in this case the building on the right, allowed me to make informed decisions about the level of the midtones. Some of the blue of the sky and the warm colours were to survive right through to completion of the painting.

Once I was happy with the areas of darkest tone I began to build up midtone areas. I painted in shadowy areas of the Basilica and brushed warm colour into the foreground to give the feeling of recession from warm back to cool.

AN URBAN LANDSCAPE

I began to accumulate some figures and firmed up the perspective in the foreground. I reworked over some of the transparent first washes to build up strong, solid colour, especially in the foreground. As I did so I identified the areas that were to be very tight and finished and those that were to remain loose and diffuse.

At the foot of the tower, figures are scurrying through into the shaft of light shining between the buildings. They are very sketchily laid in because they are only figures on the periphery of the scene and are not an important part of the painting.

St Mark's Square, Venice
38 x 42 cm (15 x 21 in)

I finished the painting by putting in all the architectural detail and defining the flagpoles. I adjusted some of the darks to make them lighter and vice versa, particularly in the foreground, where I put in opaque white to make it less heavy.

These figures are painted in enough detail for them to be identifiable as tourists, one carrying a camera with visible strap round his neck. This high degree of detail is set against the sumptuous texture of the light as it floods out of the Basilica door and is reflected in the wet foreground. The whole painting is about balancing hard and soft edges, high detail and soft recessive areas.

STILL LIFE

A still life can be as simple or as complex as you choose to make it, and the objects it is composed of can come from nature, industry or your own domestic life. Some of the most delightful still lifes are just a simple arrangement of food, either on a table prepared for a meal or in the kitchen waiting to be cooked; fruit and vegetables provide a range of surfaces and colours for you to explore. With still life you have complete control over the objects and how they are placed, and if you want to do a floral study you can make it one of an ornate vase carrying lush, complex blooms or just a couple of daisies in a plain little jug.

This is an exploratory sketch of a little vase of flowers, placed centrally but with darker and stronger tones and colours on the left to make a more interesting diagonal composition. The drawing was done with a biro, which is a quick and friendly medium for sketching. I then brushed on some colour to see how things were placed.

The overall shape the vase makes is a rectangular composition, but I decided to go for one that more closely approaches a square. I started with loose washes of colour that mainly established the edges present within the painting.

I worked up the strength of the colour throughout and increased the drawing. Only a loose and impressionistic painting, this still life could be worked up still further or left as it is in the form of a less finished picture.

The lights have been worked up to make the glass look transparent, while the blue on the left becomes a reduced tone.

The rim of the vase shows what an extreme tonal range you can encounter even in something as clear as glass.

FIGURES

Figures give scale and narrative to a scene and you will often want to include them in your pictures. Unless they are playing a major role you need to show very little detail; as long as you can sketch a recognizable posture the viewer's imagination will do the rest for you. Stand in front of a mirror and watch how any movement you make with one part of your body will cause an opposite reaction in another.

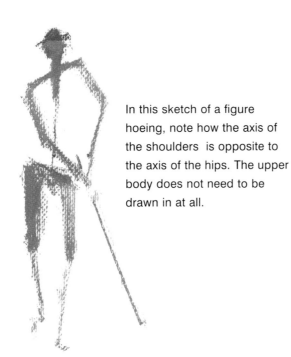

In this sketch of a figure hoeing, note how the axis of the shoulders is opposite to the axis of the hips. The upper body does not need to be drawn in at all.

Without the little figure standing at its foot to give scale, the viewer would have no idea as to whether this was a tall tree or a sapling.

I drew these marathon runners without taking my pen off the paper, keeping it constantly moving. This continuous line drawing does not try to capture any detail, only the essence of figures running.

EXTERIOR AND INTERIOR FIGURES

Your figures may be populating a large urban space in an impersonal fashion or perhaps occupying an intimate corner of a restaurant or café. Keep your sketchbook constantly with you and make notes of the narratives you can glean from people's interaction.

Make sure that figures standing in groups make an interesting shape as a single entity. Look for small figures seen beyond large ones to give variety of size and strength of tone.

In this intimate café scene the light is coming from behind the figure in the red dress and catching on the shoulder of the figure with its back to us. The profusion of plants adds vigour to the painting.

FIGURES

LIFE DRAWING

If you feel you would like to embark on more stringent drawing of the human form, sign up for a local life drawing class. Life drawing has always been the acknowledged way of training an artist's eye, brain and hand and as a means of learning how to subtly model with line, tone and colour it cannot be beaten.

This detailed drawing by Gaynor Lloyd is concerned with establishing the form of the figure. Note the subtle relationship between the angle of the hips and shoulders and how the weight is thrown on one leg.

Here Gaynor Lloyd's drawing examines where the main areas of tone lie but handles them in a loose way. They hint at very strong light sources coming in from several angles to describe extremely complex forms.

Again the tonal areas have been examined but this time the artist has used colour. Note the subtle recession in the thrust-forward leg created by the blues changing from warm to cool as the shin tilts back.

A BEACH LANDSCAPE

The seaside is an ideal place to sketch people at rest and at play and to set them in the context of a landscape. If you take oil paints to the beach, you will need to make sure that you keep them clear of sand or you risk ruined tubes of paint. Watercolour sketches that can be translated to oils back in the studio are a better choice if you will be working near people kicking up dry sand.

This little pen and wash sketch is a preliminary look at composition to establish where the horizon might be and to explore the tonal values.

To try out some colour ideas I used watercolour pigments for speed. The light on the sea was achieved by reserving white paper, a necessary technique with watercolour but one I thought I might also use with oils later.

I liked the exuberance of the colour, so back in the studio I decided to paint my beach scene in oils. The relaxed figures having a picnic are in strong contrast to the smaller but more vigorous figures seen in the distance. In the background, the colours change from warm to cool as they traverse from left to right. This is echoed in the figures by using predominantly warm colour in the picnickers and much cooler blues and even grey skin tones in the background figures. The trees act as a framing device, bringing the seated figures further into the foreground.

The handling of the trees is done with the same vigour as that of the figures, in keeping with the feel of the scene.

The figures with the ball are sketched in very lightly, allowing the viewer to gather information just from their postures.

The seated figures are much more closely observed; note the subtle changes of colour on the woman's arms.

LIGHT AND WEATHER

As artists, we can derive a lot of visual stimulation from what nature throws at us. Howling autumn winds and lashing rain give the chance to capture the movement of storm-tossed trees and exciting reflections, so don't feel that if the weather is bad there is no aesthetic point to going out. Misty mornings and hazy sunsets offer a different challenge in the handling of diffuse effects, while bright sunshine calls for vibrant colour.

St Theodore Atop His Arch,
St Mark's Square
35.5 x 46 cm (14 x 18 in)
The light in Venice can be very harsh, but on this day it was diffuse and pearly, with a lot of reflected light coming from the water. The emphasis of that softness is heightened by the hard lines in the foreground and the stark colour on the overhang of the building.

Looking West up the Grand Canal
76 x 117 cm (30 x 46 in)
The approach to the atmospherics in this picture is similar to that above but the colour is much more close-toned and muted, giving a more gentle, restful feel. There is very little middle distance in the painting and the stimulus comes from reading it sideways from one tone and colour to the next rather than looking at very obvious recession.

Drying Out the Nets
30.5 x 41 cm (12 x 16 in)

After a hard day working at sea the fishermen have pulled up their boat on the shingled beach and are drying their nets while a storm threatens from the east. Storms provide tonal drama and a sense of movement in the sky.

The stormy marks in the sky were rubbed out with a rag to make them very soft and recessive. They direct the eye to the high drama of the dark figure and the light catching the wet nets.

THE SEASONS

The changing seasons call for different handling of colour and light and for different equipment on outings too. A hat and an umbrella to shield your eyes from glare on hot sunny days is essential, while in winter you will benefit from a handwarmer if you are attempting any more than the quickest sketch.

Spring Growth in Syracuse
35.5 x 38 cm (14 x 15 in)
The fresh colours of spring in a square in Syracuse are captured by the pastel shades of the stuccoed café and by Chrome Green used almost straight from the tube.

The Acropolis, Early Morning 25.5 x 35.5 cm (10 x 14 in)
The glowing light of the rising summer sun can present dramatic compositions. Here the brightly lit face of the Acropolis disappears into purply shadows in flat tones that contrast with the textural busyness of the palm trees.

Admiralty Arch in the Rain, London
35.5 x 45 cm (14 x 18 in)
The Admiralty Arch seen at twilight on a rainy day conjures up the atmosphere of an autumnal city. Rain always presents the most interesting foregrounds and the little colour notes in the reflections bring the vertical composition right down to meet us at the bottom of the painting.

Much of the colour in the painting was provided by the cool blue underpainting. The figures, though barely described, speak of people huddled up against the cold and struggling to keep their footing.

Trams in the Snow, Switzerland 122 × 122 cm (48 × 48 in)
For this chilly Swiss scene I added a slight blue tint to the primer to enhance the coldness of the snow against the warmer colour of the sky.

USING PHOTOGRAPHS

Taking photographs is a good way of recording information, but you should never copy directly from them and you will tend to do this if you have them next to you. If you are using one for detail, put it at the far end of the studio so that you have to walk over to see it. Take little bits of information and make them your own as you walk back so that your painting will be an interpretation rather than a copy. Pin up photographs taken for tone and colour at a distance where you can see just big slabs of tone and high points of colour.

To sharpen up your eye, take your camera out with you with a specific purpose in mind. One day might be devoted to photographing linear subjects, for example, where you look for light lines on dark, dark lines on light, geometric lines and so forth. Spend a day on tonal relationships, moving in very close to objects so that you lose all sense of what they are and, in the manner of an artist, look instead at lines, surfaces and textures. If you find this difficult, taking the photographs slightly out of focus will help.

Looking out for linear subjects, I was pleased to find these shadows from a pergola making soft, curved lines across a concrete seat and developing into hard geometric lines on the path.

On this fairground carousel the linear interest was in the light-coloured lines seen against a dark background.

This photograph is all about colour, with the reflection of a red boat among floating mussel shells in the water outside a café in Minorca.

I took this photograph through the wing of a swan, with the light shining through it from the back. I was looking for subtlety of design in nature and found an image about soft texture too.

Using a photograph or a postcard, you can trace off an area to reduce a complex scene to simple tones. Put two sheets of tracing paper over it to cut out the midtones. Tracing off the dark areas will help you to decide how to lay your first washes of light and dark tones.

I took a photograph of this colourful scene and laid a white strip across it to see how dark the tones were. The sea and sky are often thought to be much lighter than they are in reality.

LOOKING FOR RHYTHMS

Looking for rhythms in your subject and translating them to your painting can bring unity to your compositions and can also arouse an emotional response in the viewer. Rhythms arise through the repetition of certain elements, the echoing shapes of objects or the spaces between them, and the recurrence of line, colour and tone in balance with each other. Employing an overall directional movement is another way to give rhythm to your work.

Shown in extremes of tone, the painting by Stubbs on p. 7 reveals itself to have strong diagonal rhythms that emphasize the drama of the moment.

Blues, greys and subtle greens are cool, relaxing colours. Sinuous horizontal curves are equally calming. Combined here, they make soft flowing rhythms that carry a sense of peace.

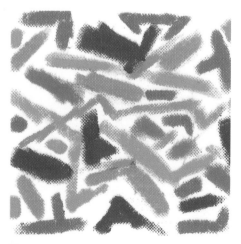

Zigzag, staccato lines express agitation and restlessness. When they are drawn in hot reds and high tones of other warm colours, the rhythms become increasingly jarring and anxious.

MAN-MADE SHAPES

There is often the temptation to think that the natural world must offer the most beautiful subject matter, but as artists we look at texture, light, line and colour and these can be equally interesting on an old rusting piece of machinery or a modernistic building rising above a cramped and noisy street. Including man-made objects in your painting inevitably adds a touch of interesting narrative, for even if figures cannot be seen we know they have been present.

This moored wooden boat gave me an opportunity to explore warm brown and violet reflections in the water, the brushstrokes expressing the movement of the current on which it was floating.

For a quick sketch of a Welsh barn, I used large slabs of tone and complementary colour. They give a geometric composition that could easily become an abstract painting.

The strong shape of this big viaduct makes a powerful composition. Its industrial nature emphasizes the domesticity of the village huddled behind it.

BRINGING IT ALL TOGETHER

My painting of the church of Santa Maria della Salute in Venice may strike you as very complex in its subject of classical architecture and reflections in the Grand Canal. However, all paintings share the same beginnings of decisions about composition, format and tone, followed by the first simple washes. If you get these right, you have laid the basis for a good painting which you can develop as far as you wish to.

I began with a little study in oils, using a warm palette to see if a feeling of vitality would suit the subject and what I wanted to say about it.

Next I tried a cooler palette to give a calmer mood and altered the composition, bringing in the buildings on the lefthand side so that they occupied nearly a quarter of the painting.

Deciding that I preferred the second composition, I now did a very loose version in watercolour to see what might arise. Because watercolour is immediate and easy to use, this is commonly done by artists planning an oil painting. These preliminary sketches are never a waste of time; they help you start the painting proper confident about what you are trying to do.

Working on MDF board prepared with acrylic primer, I laid in my initial colours with a large housepainter's brush. These first washes are crucial because they set the whole tone of the picture. The lefthand side of the painting is already starting to develop as strong colour where the light is hitting the buildings from the right.

I had painted in the buildings on the far right almost in silhouette so the source of light was already strongly established even before I began to indicate it on the water. At this stage I was repainting over the first thin glazes of colour with much more full-bodied paint to establish some areas of final colour.

I now began more detailed work, such as identifying the boats more strongly and indicating individual waves. I strengthened everything up, putting stronger colour on the roofs and darkening the recessive areas on the left to make the light work well.

BRINGING IT ALL TOGETHER

In this detail from the finished painting, you can see that the most distant building is a very simple soft-edged glaze of blues pulled together with some grey linework put in with a rigger. Beyond that, the Lido is painted with very soft-edged brushwork.

Santa Maria della Salute from the Grand Canal, Venice 76 x 122 cm (30 x 48 in)

In the foreground, the movement of the water is described by energetic, rhythmic brushwork. Not every wave is painted in detail since this would distract attention from the main focus of interest, which is the far-distant warmth as we look down the Grand Canal. Note how the linework recedes in strength from the foreground to the distance.